CUNY Testing Program

Characteristics, Results, and Implications for Policy and Research

STEPHEN P. KLEIN

MARIA ORLANDO

Supported by the Council for Aid to Education

RAND

This report is based on research undertaken by RAND and its subsidiary, the Council for Aid to Education, under contract to The Mayor's Task Force on the City University of New York. Additional funding was provided by The Achelis Foundation, The Bodman Foundation, The William & Flora Hewlett Foundation, The J. M. Kaplan Foundation, The John M. Olin Foundation, The David and Lucile Packard Foundation, and The Starr Foundation.

ISBN: 0-8330-2908-8

RAND is a nonprofit institution that helps improve policy and decisionmaking through research and analysis. RAND® is a registered trademark. RAND's publications do not necessarily reflect the opinions or policies of its research sponsors.

Published 2000 by RAND
1700 Main Street, P.O. Box 2138, Santa Monica, CA 90407-2138
1200 South Hayes Street, Arlington, VA 22202-5050
RAND URL: http://www.rand.org/
To order RAND documents or to obtain additional information, contact Distribution Services: Telephone: (310) 451-7002; Fax: (310) 451-6915; E-Mail: order@rand.org

In May 1998, Rudolph W. Giuliani, the mayor of New York City, convened an Advisory Task Force on the City University of New York (CUNY). This task force asked the Council for Aid to Education (a subsidiary of RAND) to conduct an independent analysis of several aspects of CUNY's policies and procedures.

This report responds to the task force's request for information about the quality of the tests CUNY uses to decide who must take remedial courses. These tests play an important role at CUNY. The pass/fail decisions that are based on them result in a very large percentage of its freshmen being required to take remedial courses in reading, writing, and/or mathematics (about 65 percent of the students seeking bachelor's degrees and nearly 90 percent of those seeking associate degrees fall into this category). Hence, a large portion of CUNY's resources and its students' time is devoted to remedial instruction. This report also provides a statistical profile of CUNY's incoming freshmen, presents information about the relationships among various test scores and grades at CUNY, and discusses the implications of our findings.

CUNY is the third largest public university system in the United States (after California State University and the State University of New York). It also is the largest urban system. Consequently, our findings regarding the characteristics of the students at this university and its procedures for determining who receives remedial instruction are likely to be of interest to policymakers at other urban public higher education institutions across the United States.

A previous RAND report that was prepared for the task force examined CUNY's governance structure, how this structure contributes to the university's problems, and how it might be changed to improve performance (Gill, 2000; The Task Force, 1999). That report also provided the historical background, information about school characteristics, and related context for RAND's work at CUNY.

CONTENTS

FIGURES

TABLES

Remedial instruction at the City University of New York (CUNY) consumes a substantial amount of instructional resources and student time. Roughly 65 percent of CUNY's bachelor degree students and nearly 90 percent of its associate degree students are required to take remedial courses in reading, writing, and/or mathematics. In response to a request from the Mayor's Advisory Task Force on CUNY's programs and governance, we examined the tests this university uses to determine which students must take remedial instruction. We also examined a number of related issues, including the academic ability and other characteristics of its incoming freshman students.

CUNY uses the following three tests to determine whether an incoming freshman requires remedial instruction: the Reading Assessment Test (RAT), the Mathematics Assessment Test (MAT), and the Writing Assessment Test (WAT). These tests are collectively referred to as the Freshman Skills Assessment Test or FSAT. The RAT and MAT are multiple-choice exams. The WAT is a single-question essay test.

TECHNICAL CHARACTERISTICS

The RAT and MAT had adequate score reliabilities; i.e., the pass/fail decisions that were based on these two tests were not seriously affected by chance. That was not the case with the WAT even though this test was the major determinant of who was required to receive remedial instruction.

There was some empirical support for the construct validity of the RAT and MAT; i.e., these tests correlated well with SAT-Verbal and

SAT-Math scores, respectively. However, the three tests in the FSAT, by themselves, had fairly low criterion-related validity coefficients (i.e., they did not do a very good job in predicting first-year grades). We suspect this was due, at least in part, to the low reliability of the first-year grades. For example, because so many students were receiving nongraded remedial instruction, their first-year grade point averages (GPAs) were often based on just a few courses.

There was no documentation regarding how the FSAT passing scores were set. This is a particularly serious concern with the WAT because the question is changed each time this exam is given and the results have a major impact on whether a student is required to receive remedial instruction.

We looked for but did not find any evidence of racial/ethnic bias in the FSAT scores. In fact, minority students earned somewhat lower first-year GPAs than would be expected on the basis of their FSAT scores and the relationship between FSAT scores and first-year GPAs for nonminority students.

CHARACTERISTICS OF CUNY FRESHMEN

Analyses of the cohort of 1997 incoming freshmen indicate that about 65 percent of the bachelor degree students and nearly 90 percent of the associate degree students failed one or more of the FSATs and therefore were required to receive remedial instruction. Minority students make up about 80 percent of the incoming class. Roughly half of all the incoming freshmen are classified as "English-language learners" (as distinct from "English speakers").

Whereas almost all the incoming freshmen had taken FSATs, only about half had taken SATs. We used the relationship between SAT and FSAT scores among those who took both tests to impute the missing SATs. This step enabled us to compute SAT scores for each college and racial/ethnic group, which in turn allowed us to compare these scores with those earned nationally. Not surprisingly, this analysis found that English speakers generally earned higher scores than English-language learners and that within each of these two groups, white and Asian students usually earned higher scores than their classmates. Nevertheless, there was a substantial overlap in score distributions among the groups. These trends held for both bachelor degree and associate degree students.[1]

One of the more important findings for weighing policy options is that about 75 percent of all the incoming bachelor degree students at CUNY had SAT total scores (verbal + math) that were below the presumptive national average for all takers. We also found rather large differences in average FSAT and SAT scores among the different CUNY colleges. These differences in input were not matched by corresponding differences in first-year GPAs. This finding indicates that grading standards were not consistent across the senior colleges let alone between the associate and bachelor degree programs.

MULTIPLE PREDICTORS OF FRESHMEN GRADES

Certain combinations of variables were able to predict first-year GPAs at CUNY far more accurately than was possible when these same variables were used individually. For example, after controlling for the student's CUNY college, primary language, and degree sought (bachelor versus associate), the combination of high school grade point average (HSGPA) and SAT scores provided a prediction of a student's first-year grades that was about four times more accurate than predictions based on the RAT or MAT alone. Moreover, the level of accuracy achieved with this combination of variables was slightly higher than what is typically obtained at other colleges. In this context, predictive accuracy is indicated by the percentage of variance explained.

ADDITIONAL RESEARCH ACTIVITIES

We identified several areas in which CUNY should consider conducting further work and research. These areas include efforts to improve the quality of the data it collects on each student, explore ways to make better use of HSGPA in admissions and placement, establish appropriate pass/fail standards for the FSAT (if CUNY decides to retain this set of tests), examine the source of the large disparities in

---

[1]Some senior colleges offer both bachelor and associate degrees, while all non-senior colleges offer only associate degrees (see Table 3.4 for details).

grading standards among the CUNY colleges, evaluate the effectiveness of different remedial programs at CUNY, and investigate the "value added" of a CUNY degree.

POLICY OPTIONS AND RECOMMENDATIONS

CUNY is at a crossroads. It can continue with its very modest admission standards and allocation of substantial resources to remedial instruction, or it can raise standards at some or all of its colleges. If it adopts the first strategy, then we strongly urge CUNY to improve the process of determining who is required to get remedial instruction. We also recommend that CUNY investigate whether those who receive this instruction truly develop the skills and abilities that are essential for college-level work.

We further recommend that CUNY require all students to take the SAT so that there is an external, independent, and standardized benchmark of student ability. This is essential for an analysis of the effects of any changes in CUNY's admissions, promotion, graduation, and education policies.

Finally, if CUNY decides to tighten admission standards at some or all of its colleges, then it should do this on the basis of a student's HSGPA and SAT scores. New York State Regents scores also may be considered. However, because these measures (and particularly the tests) may have a disparate impact, CUNY should monitor closely the effect of any changes in admissions policies. In the long run, this approach may lead to CUNY graduating more truly qualified minority students than it does under its current policies.

Several individuals contributed to the preparation of this report. First, we wish to thank the members of the CUNY community for their assistance and cooperation. The support and interest of Interim Deputy Chancellor Patricia Hassett and Vice Chancellor Louise Mirrer were particularly helpful in facilitating our communication with others at CUNY and in providing information that helped us understand CUNY's procedures. Dr. David Crook from the CUNY Office of Institutional Research and Analysis worked diligently and continuously with us, ensuring that we received the data we requested as well as the information necessary to decipher their contents. Dr. Donna Morgan and Deans Audrey Blumberg, Russell Hotzler, and Lester Jacobs at CUNY were also instrumental in providing valuable information and documentation.

We would also like to thank Wayne Camera at the College Entrance Examination Board for sharing his insights on the interpretation and implications of some of our findings regarding CUNY's testing program. Sally Renfro, Allison Armour-Garb, and Miriam Cilo of the Mayor's Advisory Task Force staff helped address logistic problems inherent in long-distance collaborations, and also provided useful comments on earlier versions of this report. Our thanks also goes to Amy De Cillia in the New York office of the Council for Aid to Education, who provided research support and served as RAND's New York liaison with the task force staff. Other RAND input included programming support provided by Carol Edwards, and thoughtful reviews of earlier versions of this report from Brian Stecher.

ACRONYMS

CAE	Council for Aid to Education
CUNY	City University of New York
ETS	Educational Testing Service
FSAT	Freshman Skills Assessment Test
GPA	grade point average
HSGPA	high school grade point average
MAT	Mathematics Assessment Test
RAT	Reading Assessment Test
SAT	Scholastic Assessment Test
SAT-M	SAT-Math
SAT-V	SAT-Verbal
WAT	Writing Assessment Test

Chapter One

INTRODUCTION

This report describes research that was conducted for The Mayor's Advisory Task Force on the City University of New York (CUNY). This task force was charged with reviewing, examining, and making recommendations regarding (1) the uses of New York City funding by CUNY, (2) the effects of open admissions and remedial education on CUNY and on CUNY's capacity to provide college-level courses and curricula of high quality to its students, (3) the best means of arranging for third parties to provide remediation services to ensure that prospective CUNY students can perform college-level work prior to their admission to CUNY, and (4) the implementation of other reform measures as may be appropriate.

The task force asked the Council for Aid to Education (CAE), a subsidiary of RAND, to conduct an independent analysis of several aspects of the task force's mission. The first report RAND prepared for the task force examined CUNY's governance structure, how this structure contributes to the university's problems, and how it might be changed to improve performance (Gill, 2000; The Task Force, 1999). That report also provided the historical background, information about school characteristics, and related context for RAND's work at CUNY.

This report focuses mainly on the tests CUNY uses to decide who should receive remedial instruction and in what subjects. These tests play an important role at CUNY because they lead to about 65 percent of its freshman bachelor degree students and nearly 90 percent of its freshman associate degree students being required to take remedial courses in reading, writing, and/or mathematics.

These high percentages are probably by-products of the K–12 educational system in New York, CUNY's essentially open admissions policies, decisions about where to place passing scores on CUNY's tests, and other factors. However, regardless of the reasons, it is evident that CUNY is currently devoting a large portion of its resources and its students' time to remedial instruction.

Because remedial instruction has such a central role at CUNY, the task force wanted an analysis of the quality of the tests CUNY uses to determine who receives this instruction, including the appropriateness of the pass/fail scores on these measures. Chapter Two of this report responds to the task force's request by examining the extent to which the CUNY tests produce scores that are reliable, valid, and fair to all students. We also explore the cost-effectiveness of CUNY's testing program. Chapter Three provides a statistical picture of the incoming freshmen at CUNY. These students' characteristics must be factored into CUNY's policy decisions regarding admissions standards and the different missions of its colleges. Chapter Four investigates the relationships among high school grades, freshman grades at CUNY, and scores on other measures (including CUNY's tests and the College Board's Scholastic Assessment Test, the SAT). Chapter Five discusses some additional activities and research that CUNY could conduct to help inform policy decisions. Chapter Six presents our conclusions and considers the policy implications of our findings.

Chapter Two

ANALYSIS OF THE CUNY TESTING PROGRAM

The CUNY testing program uses three tests to determine which students require remedial instruction. The Reading Assessment Test (RAT) contains 45 multiple-choice questions. The form currently being used by CUNY has a passing score of 30. The Mathematics Assessment Test (MAT) has two sections. The first section is used for making remedial placement decisions. It has 40 multiple-choice items. A score of 25 or higher on this section is required for passing. There are seven forms of this section of the MAT (but each school decides which form to give when). On the Writing Assessment Test (WAT), students are given a choice between two questions to answer. They have 50 minutes to respond to the question they pick. Two new questions are asked each time the test is given. Two readers grade each answer on a 6-point scale. A total score of 8 or higher summed over the two readings is required for passing.

We obtained student demographic and academic information files from the CUNY Office of Institutional Research and Analysis. From these files, we identified 25,436 students who were first-time entering freshmen in the fall of 1997. We deleted the 4 percent of these students (N=1,007) who did not have any FSAT scores on record. Thus, our analyses are based on the remaining 24,429 students who had at least one FSAT score on file.

Table 2.1 shows the mean score, standard deviation, and percent passing on each test in the cohort of incoming students in 1997. In this cohort, 65 percent of the students seeking a bachelor's degree failed at least one test, 38 percent failed at least two, and 13 percent failed all three. The corresponding percentages among students

Table 2.1

Mean, Standard Deviation, and Percent Passing in Fall 1997

Test	Bachelor Degree ($N = 8,705$)			Associate Degree ($N = 15,493$)		
	Mean	SD[a]	% Passing	Mean	SD	% Passing
RAT	31.23	7.60	62	26.68	8.09	39
MAT	29.20	6.92	74	22.20	7.74	39
WAT	6.83	1.60	48	6.10	1.63	29
Total	67.32	12.97	35	55.45	13.51	12

NOTE: Because of missing data, mean total does not equal sum of RAT, MAT, and WAT scores. Total percent passing equals the percentage of students passing all three tests.

[a]SD = standard deviation.

seeking an associate degree were 88 percent, 68 percent, and 37 percent. Only 35 percent of the bachelor students and 12 percent of the associate students passed all three tests.

The remainder of this chapter discusses the reliability, validity, fairness, and costs of the three CUNY tests. We also contrast these characteristics with those of the SATs.

RELIABILITY

Reliability is usually reported on a scale from 0 to 1.00, where the higher the number, the greater the degree to which an individual student's relative standing (e.g., percentile rank) on one form of the test is consistent with that student's standing on another form of that test.

Determining the reliability of a test score typically involves measuring the consistency in student performance across the test's questions. In general, longer tests (as measured by the number of questions asked) have higher score reliabilities than shorter tests. Our computations of the reliability of the RAT and MAT were based on the scores earned by a sample of 1997 incoming freshmen (first-time takers). These analyses found that both of these tests had a reliability of .89, which is reasonably high for tests of this length. For example, the estimated reliability for the somewhat longer SAT-Math (SAT-M) and SAT-Verbal (SAT-V) ranges from .91 to .94 (College Board, 1999).

Several factors (besides the number of questions each student answers) influence the reliability of essay tests. One of the factors is the extent to which different graders assign the same score to an answer. This is called "inter-reader consistency." Another factor is the degree to which the questions measure the same thing. For example, one essay question might require a narrative response while another might require a persuasive argument. With respect to inter-reader consistency, studies done by CUNY suggest that about 15 percent of the students would have their pass/fail status on the WAT affected if a different reader graded their answers (Office of Academic Affairs, 1998).

It was not possible to determine the score reliability of the WAT because each student answers only one essay question. However, an estimate based on studies of similar single-question essay tests would be in the range of .25 to .60 (Dunbar, Koretz, and Hoover, 1991). The one essay question that is asked is in the persuasive genre. No other genres are tested.

In the context of how CUNY uses the FSATs—namely, to make pass/fail decisions—reliability should be assessed in terms of the likelihood that a student's pass/fail status on a test would remain the same regardless of which form of that test the student took. For example, would the student's pass/fail status on the WAT be affected if that student was asked an essay question that was administered to incoming freshmen in the fall of 1997 versus a question that was asked in the fall of 1998? Similarly, would a student's pass/fail status on the MAT depend on which form of that test the student took?

Table 2.2 shows the relationship among the following three factors: (1) the reliability of a test's scores (on the 0–1.00 scale), (2) the passing rate of the test (i.e., from 0% to 100%), and (3) the misclassification rate. In this context, the misclassification rate is the percentage of students whose pass/fail status on one version of a test would be different from their pass/fail status on another version of that test (i.e., the percentage of students who would be erroneously classified as passing or failing). The values in Table 2.2 were computed by Professor David Freedman of the Statistics Department at the University of California, Berkeley, using a Monte Carlo simulation study with 10,000 replications.

Table 2.2

Percentage of Students Whose Pass/Fail Status Would Be Misclassified at Various Combinations of Passing Rate and Score Reliability

Percent Passing	Score Reliability									
	.00	.10	.20	.30	.40	.50	.60	.70	.80	.90
90	19	17	17	16	14	13	12	11	9	6
80	32	30	28	27	25	23	20	17	14	10
70	42	39	37	35	31	29	25	22	17	12
60	48	45	42	39	36	32	29	25	20	14
50	50	47	44	40	37	33	30	26	21	14
40	48	45	42	39	36	32	29	25	20	14
30	42	40	38	35	32	29	26	22	18	13
20	32	30	28	27	25	23	20	18	14	10
10	19	18	16	16	15	13	12	11	09	6

Boxed area is probable range of pass/fail classification errors for the WAT.

About 60 percent to 70 percent of the bachelor degree students and 40 percent of the associate degree students pass the RAT and MAT (see Table 2.1). Both of these tests have reliabilities close to .90. Thus, each of these tests would misclassify only about 14 percent of the students. About 50 percent of the bachelor students and 30 percent of the associate students pass the WAT. The boxed area in Table 2.2 shows the probable range of misclassification rates for this test (i.e., assuming its reliability falls somewhere between .30 and .60). The misclassification rates in this zone are about 35 percent for bachelor students and 30 percent for associate students. In short, at least 25 percent (but probably more) of first-time WAT takers are erroneously categorized; i.e., they fail when they should pass or pass when they should fail.

The low score reliability of a single-question essay test stems mainly from students not being highly consistent with themselves in their writing ability across questions. In other words, a student's score is as much or more a function of the student's unique response to the particular question that is asked as it is of that student's overall ability to write. This means that a student might pass the essay question asked on the 1997 WAT but fail the one asked on the 1998 WAT while another student could easily have the opposite experience. The limited data that are available regarding inter-reader consistency on the WAT suggest that readers generally agree with each other in the score they assign to an answer. Hence, inter-reader consistency is probably not a major source of score reliability problems.

VALIDITY

The validity of the FSATs for making initial placement decisions is measured by how well they distinguish between the students who truly do and do not need remedial instruction. To be valid, scores must first be reliable. Thus, reliability is a necessary but not sufficient condition for validity (which is why we are so concerned about the WAT). However, reliability alone does not ensure validity. Scores must also reflect the abilities the tests are designed to measure.

We examined two indicators of the FSAT's validity; namely, (1) how well the scores on these tests correlate with scores on other similar and dissimilar tests (this is a type of "construct" validity) and (2) how well the FSAT scores predict a student's grade point average (GPA) at CUNY (this is called "predictive" validity). An appropriate measure of a student's success in remedial programs was not available.

Construct Validity

We obtained Scholastic Assessment Test (SAT) scores for 5,153 (59 percent) of the 8,705 entering bachelor degree students and for 3,632 (23 percent) of the 15,493 entering associate degree students in 1997. Overall, about 36 percent of the CUNY students had SAT scores. Roughly half of these scores were for students who had asked the Educational Testing Service (ETS) to send their scores to CUNY. The other half were obtained from the College Board Corporation as part of a special study (CUNY does not require students to take the SATs and students may have to pay a nominal fee to have their SAT scores sent to a college).

The pattern of correlations among SAT and FSAT scores is consistent with what would be expected if the FSATs measured what they purported to measure. Table 2.3 shows that SAT-V scores correlated higher with RAT scores than with MAT scores while the reverse was true for SAT-M scores. These findings provide some support for the construct validity of the RAT and MAT; i.e., these tests appear to measure reading and mathematical skills, respectively. It is not clear

Table 2.3

Correlation Between SAT and FSAT Scores

Correlation Between	Bachelor Degree	Associate Degree	Total
SAT-V and RAT	.68	.53	.65
SAT-M and MAT	.66	.50	.65
SAT-V and MAT	.36	.23	.38
SAT-M and RAT	.41	.26	.42
SAT-V and SAT-M	.57	.50	.59
RAT and MAT	.38	.34	.42

why the correlation between SAT-V and SAT-M scores was higher than the correlation between RAT and MAT scores, particularly since there was some restriction in the range of SAT scores (the more able students, as indicated by their FSATs, were somewhat more likely to take the SATs than other students).

Predictive Validity

We explored the predictive validity of the FSAT and SAT scores by assessing how well these scores correlated with the CUNY students' GPAs. Table 2.4 shows the mean validity coefficients for CUNY as a whole weighted by the number of students in each school. The total FSAT score in these analyses is the sum of the students' RAT, MAT, and WAT scores. All of these validity coefficients have a possible range from –1 to 1, with –1 indicating a perfect negative relationship (i.e., as test score increases, GPA decreases), 0 indicating no relationship, and 1 indicating a perfect positive relationship (i.e., as test score increases, GPA increases).

Table 2.4 shows that freshman GPAs at CUNY have relatively low correlations with both SAT and FSAT scores. Nationally, the typical correlation of SAT scores with freshman year GPA is about .50 after adjustment for restriction in range (College Board, 1999). However, the appropriateness of this adjustment has been questioned in the literature (Crocker and Algina, 1986). If we had adjusted the values in Table 2.4 for bachelor degree students, the coefficients for SAT-V and SAT-M would be .22 and .38, respectively, still well below the national average.

Table 2.4

Mean Correlation with Freshman GPA at CUNY by Degree Type

	SAT Scores			FSAT Scores			
Degree Type	Verbal	Math	Total	RAT	MAT	WAT	Total
Bachelor	.19	.24	.25	.18	.25	.14	.25
Associate	.08	.19	.17	.06	.19	.04	.16

Table 2.5 shows the predictive validity coefficients separately by school and degree sought (bachelor or associate). We did this because of what appeared to be fairly large differences in grading standards among colleges. Specifically, there were large differences in average FSAT and SAT scores among colleges. These differences presumably reflect large differences in the average general academic

Table 2.5

Correlations with 1997–98 Freshman GPA at CUNY by Degree Sought and School

		SAT Scores			FSAT Scores			
Degree/College[a]	N	Verbal	Math	Total	RAT	MAT	WAT	Total
Bachelor								
Baruch	945	.28	.22	.29	.34	.24	.21	.37
Brooklyn	1,222	.27	.33	.33	.21	.32	.16	.30
City College	844	.18	.23	.24	.12	.21	.17	.20
Hunter	1,550	.10	.23	.19	.08	.27	.06	.20
John Jay	807	.09	.14	.13	.09	.18	.09	.16
Lehman	639	.14	.21	.20	.17	.22	.12	.24
Queens	1,096	.21	.23	.26	.21	.22	.16	.27
Staten Island	230	.24	.24	.30	.28	.32	.21	.39
York	414	.20	.29	.30	.14	.28	.10	.25
Associate								
Bronx	874	.14	.26	.22	.12	.26	.08	.21
Hostos	543	−.02	.09	.15	.00	.11	.08	.18
John Jay	594	.03	.15	.10	.04	.17	.05	.13
Kingsborough	1,618	.19	.26	.28	.21	.29	.12	.31
La Guardia[b]	1,884	−.03	.17	.07	−.03	.20	−.04	.09
Manhattan	2,483	.01	.19	.11	.00	.19	.00	.11
Medgar Evers	423	.16	.23	.25	.18	.26	.14	.27
NYC Technical	1,738	.03	.17	.11	.02	.15	.02	.10
Queensborough	1,341	.11	.19	.18	.11	.20	.05	.19
Staten Island	1,131	.22	.18	.25	.23	.22	.18	.29

[a]Results are reported for each degree/college combination with over 50 students.
[b]Correlations based on fall semester GPA only because spring data were missing.

abilities of their students. However, these differences did not correspond to the differences in these colleges' mean average first-year grades (see Table 3.4 for details).

The validity coefficients in Tables 2.4 and 2.5 are fairly low, especially for associate students. These coefficients may be depressed because of reliability problems with the students' GPAs. Specifically, the GPAs of many freshmen were based on just a few courses. Officially, part-timers comprised 9 percent of the bachelor students and 14 percent of the associate students.

Despite these modest part-timer rates, first-year GPAs for half of the bachelor students are based on less than 22 credit hours (about seven courses). Half of the freshmen associate students had less than 14 credit hours. This situation probably stemmed from many students taking remedial courses that did not count in the computation of credit hours toward GPA. The standard deviations of their SAT-V and SAT-M scores were close to those in the population of all takers nationally. Hence, the modest validity coefficients in Tables 2.4 and 2.5 cannot be explained by restrictions in the range of ability of the students tested.

Pass/Fail Scores

It is not clear whether the FSAT passing scores are appropriate. We are not alone in this judgment. The CUNY administration has been advised by others to study the appropriateness of the passing scores (e.g., Otheguy, 1990), but to our knowledge, it has not systematically done so. Valid use of tests requires meaningful and defensible passing scores. For example, although RAT scores have a low positive correlation with first-semester GPA, there is no evidence that students who score below the passing score on the RAT are not prepared for credit-bearing college courses, or that students who score at or above it are prepared.

The appropriateness of the cut score becomes even more serious when we consider the WAT. This test has the lowest technical quality, but the most real impact. Students who fail it are generally regarded by CUNY faculty as truly lacking in writing ability. In addition, more students fail this test than fail the RAT or MAT (see Table 2.1). It is possible that the passing scores on the FSATs separate students into two distinct groups in terms of readiness for college courses. However, results of a pilot study conducted by the CUNY administration suggest that students with a score of 6 on the WAT may do as well in college courses as those who pass with a score of 8. Moreover, CUNY has not used any statistical methods to examine— let alone control for—the effect of varying difficulty in essay questions from year to year. The same goes for possible differences over time in average reader leniency. Hence, it may be more difficult to earn a score of "8" one year than another.

The lack of controlled, systematic research into the appropriateness of the passing scores is a serious problem for the validity of the tests. Based on personal communications with CUNY faculty, we have the impression that a number of small-scale cut score studies have been conducted throughout the history of CUNY's testing program. Unfortunately, verbal descriptions and references to results of previous cut score studies cannot be taken at face value because little is known about the quality of the design and analyses in these studies. More research of this type must be performed and well documented so that cut scores and their consequences can be examined.

How Scores Are Used

The FSATs were originally intended to serve as a gatekeeper to upper division courses at the senior-level colleges. However, starting in about 1978, they were used systemwide as a mechanism for placing students in remedial courses. Some colleges also apparently use them to assess a student's progress in remediation, but this strategy may not be appropriate given the concerns that have been raised about the breaches in the security of the FSATs. CUNY was unable to provide validity evidence for any of the tests' purposes. Indeed, to our knowledge, the only systematic analysis of the validity of FSAT scores is contained in this report and our data apply only to their possible use as a predictor of first-year grades. Our data do not speak directly to whether the FSAT scores are valid for the major purpose for which these scores are used; namely, deciding who needs remedial instruction.

FAIRNESS

Several factors need to be considered in evaluating the fairness of a testing program. Our evaluation focused on racial/ethnic bias, test security, setting passing scores, and the decisions based on these scores. There are, of course, other fairness issues that we did not investigate. For example, we are not certain that the tests are appropriate for students who do not speak English as their primary language. We also did not explore whether the testing program was just as appropriate for older students as it was for younger ones. These and similar concerns can and should be addressed, but it was not possible for us to do so within the constraints of our study.

Racial/Ethnic Bias

We examined whether FSAT and SAT scores tended to over- or under-predict the grades of students in various racial/ethnic groups. In accordance with standard psychometric practice (AERA, APA, NCME, 1985), we investigated this matter by using the data on all students to construct an equation to predict freshman grades on the basis of test scores. For the reasons discussed in Chapter Three of this report, this equation also included whether the student's primary language was or was not English. Next, we computed each student's "residual" score using the formula:

$$\text{Residual Score} = \text{Actual GPA} - \text{Predicted GPA.}$$

In the context of this analysis, a test is considered "biased" against a group if its mean residual score is positive (i.e., if the mean of its actual observed GPA is greater than what would be predicted on the basis of its placement test scores). A test would be "biased" in favor of a group if the opposite occurred (i.e., if its mean residual score was negative).

Our analyses found the FSATs and SATs were not biased against Hispanic or black students. On both of these measures, the mean residual scores of the students in these groups were actually less than zero (see the appendix for details). This finding indicates that on the average, the college grades of CUNY's Hispanic and black students were lower than what would be expected on the basis of their FSAT and SAT scores. In contrast, Asian and white students tended to have positive residual scores. These results were obtained for both bachelor degree and associate degree students.

Test Security

We have been advised by reputable sources within and outside of CUNY (College Board staff and CUNY administration, including Hasset, P., and Mirrer, L., personal communications) that copies of the RAT and MAT can be purchased on the street. We had no way of determining the extent to which our population of first-time takers had access to these tests. However, FSAT and SAT scores had similar validity coefficients. This finding suggests that security is not a serious problem for first-time test takers. We suspect that a breach is likely to be more of a problem when higher stakes are attached to test outcomes; i.e., when the tests are used to decide whether a student has passed a remedial course or when they are used in the college admissions process.

COST

We did not conduct an in-depth analysis of the costs of CUNY's testing program. We did find that CUNY spends about $200,000 per year ($8.35 per student) just to score the answers to the WAT (each answer is graded by two and sometimes three readers). This figure refers only to the initial scoring of the WAT (i.e., it does not include grading of essays that might be administered after the completion of remedial coursework). This cost appears to be consistent with the cost of grading other essay exams (Camara, W., The College Board, personal communication). Eliminating the WAT may be opposed by the CUNY faculty who receive payment for grading the exam. Test development and administration are additional expenses for all the CUNY tests.

The SAT costs $23.00 per student, which includes test development, administration, and scoring. This fee also includes sending the results to four colleges. Fee waivers are available for students with financial need. Currently, about 35 percent of the incoming CUNY students already take the SATs (e.g., because they are applying to schools outside of CUNY). These cost considerations and the concerns about breaches in test security suggest that CUNY should explore replacing the FSAT with the SAT.

SUMMARY AND CONCLUSIONS

We evaluated the technical quality of the CUNY testing program in the following four areas: reliability, validity, fairness, and cost. We found that score reliability was satisfactory on the RAT and MAT forms we analyzed. Assuming that the cut scores CUNY uses on these tests are appropriate, then each of them would misclassify the pass/fail status of about 14 percent of the students. About half of these misclassifications involve categorizing a student as a pass when that student should be failed while the other half are errors in the opposite direction.

We could not compute the reliability of the WAT because each student answers only one essay question. However, based on other research with other essay tests, the WAT's reliability is probably in the .30–.60 range. Consequently, the WAT misclassifies the pass/fail status of about 25 percent of the associate students and 35 percent of the bachelor students. These misclassification rates are a major concern because the WAT carries so much weight in deciding who needs remedial instruction as a result of its passing rates being the lowest of the three.

FSAT scores (particularly the RAT and MAT) generally had low positive correlations with freshman GPAs for bachelor students, indicating that these scores have reasonable predictive validity for these students. The predictive validity of the FSATs is comparable to that of the SATs in this sample. However, the FSATs and the SATs have very low predictive validities for associate students.

With respect to fairness, there do not appear to be any studies of the effectiveness of the FSATs for making placement decisions, which is the primary purpose of the tests, nor could we find any empirical basis for the pass/fail cut scores. CUNY's practice of making important decisions based on a single score also is of some concern. There is no evidence of the tests being biased against black or Hispanic students.

Analysis of the test scores of the 1997 entering freshmen did not suggest that the security of the tests had been breached, at least not on a wide scale, because the correlation between FSATs and GPAs was comparable to the correlations between SATs and GPAs. We did not examine whether possible breaches in the RAT and MAT may have affected pass/fail decisions in remedial courses (i.e., been used to assess whether a student has mastered a remedial course).

Chapter Three

DEMOGRAPHICS, HIGH SCHOOL GRADES, AND SAT SCORES

The large proportion of CUNY students requiring remedial education has led to concerns about the overall academic ability of CUNY students. This section provides descriptive information about CUNY students with regard to their demographic characteristics and academic ability (as measured by their SAT and FSAT scores, high school grades, and first-year GPAs). We also provide information about the relationship between demographic groups and test scores throughout the CUNY colleges to explore the possible impact of changing policies regarding admission and remediation.

DEMOGRAPHICS

In terms of racial/ethnic background, the four largest groups of students among Fall 1997 entering freshmen at CUNY were as follows: Asians, 10 percent; African-Americans (hereafter referred to as blacks), 27 percent; non-Hispanic whites (hereafter referred to as whites), 20 percent; and Hispanics, 28 percent. Almost all of the students in the "other" group were missing a valid racial/ethnic code (see Tables 3.1 and 3.2).

About half of the entering freshmen (both bachelor's degree and associate degree students) said English was their primary language; i.e., they said they were native English speakers and/or preferred to speak in English. For the purposes of the analyses below, we classified these students as English speakers and everyone else as English-language learners. Some of the students in the latter category may in

Table 3.1

Number of Students in Each Racial/Ethnic Group by Degree Sought and Whether They Are English Speakers or Learners

	Associate Degree			Bachelor Degree			
Group	English Speakers	English Learners	Total	English Speakers	English Learners	Total	Grand Total
Asian	221	961	1,182	410	963	1,373	2,574
Black	2,999	1,720	4,719	1,129	629	1,758	6,520
Hispanic	1,703	2,848	4,551	949	1,242	2,191	6,777
White	1,752	978	2,730	1,270	951	2,221	4,980
Other	1,012	1,299	2,311	550	612	1,162	3,578
Total	7,687	7,806	15,493	4,308	4,397	8,705	24,429

Table 3.2

Percentage of Students in Each Racial/Ethnic Group by Degree Sought and Whether They Are English Speakers or Learners

	Associate Degree			Bachelor Degree			
Group	English Speakers	English Learners	Total	English Speakers	English Learners	Total	Grand Total
Asian	3	12	8	10	22	16	10
Black	39	22	30	26	14	20	27
Hispanic	22	36	29	22	28	25	28
White	23	13	18	29	22	26	20
Other	13	17	15	13	14	13	15
Total	100	100	100	100	100	100	100

fact be fluent in English, but we had no way of identifying who they were, and for them, English was a second language. Tables 3.1 and 3.2 also show that Hispanics had the largest number and percentage of English language learners.

HIGH SCHOOL GRADE POINT AVERAGE (HSGPA)

New York City public high schools graduated 29,203 students in June 1997. Of this group, 8,559 (29 percent) entered CUNY in the fall of 1997. The mean HSGPA of those who did and did not go to CUNY were 75.5 and 72.2, respectively (as computed by CUNY on a 0 to 100 point scale). The corresponding means among CUNY and non-CUNY students who took the Regents exam were 76.3 and 77.3. These data indicate that the HSGPAs of the June 1997 high school graduates who went to CUNY were similar to the HSGPAs of the June 1997 graduates who were likely to be college bound but did not go to CUNY (the standard deviation was 15 points in the group taking the Regents exam that did not go to CUNY). CUNY is not drawing from just the bottom of the New York City pool of graduates. The mean HSGPAs of the June 1997 graduates enrolling in associate degree and bachelor degree programs at CUNY were 70.0 and 80.8, respectively. The corresponding means for the June 1997 graduates going to CUNY who took the Regents exams are 71.2 and 80.8.

IMPUTING SAT SCORES

We conducted a separate analysis to estimate what the SAT scores at CUNY would be if all entering students took Part I of the SAT. This was done by calibrating the RAT and MAT scores to SAT-V and SAT-M scores, respectively, and the FSAT-Total (RAT + MAT + WAT) to the SAT-Total for the roughly 9,000 entering students in 1997 who had FSAT and SAT scores.[1] For example, 5 percent of the 9,000 students had a RAT score of 14 or less and 5 percent had a SAT-V score of 260 or less. We therefore said a RAT score of 14 was "equivalent" to a SAT-V of 260. Similarly, we set a RAT score of 17 equivalent to an SAT-V of 310 because 10 percent of the students had a RAT score of 17 or less and 10 percent had an SAT-V of 310 or less (see Appendix for details).

We repeated the process above for every 5th percentile point to create an "equi-percentile crosswalk" between the two tests. We then used this crosswalk to construct a linear regression equation for imputing a student's SAT score from that student's corresponding FSAT score for each student who did not already have an SAT score. Because the FSAT-Total included the WAT score, the sum of a student's imputed SAT-V and SAT-M scores did not always equal that student's imputed SAT-Total score.

Finally, we ran two checks on the accuracy of the links; namely, (1) that there was a strong linear relationship between an imputed SAT

---

[1]The SAT-Total was equated to the total FSATs rather than only the RAT and MAT because the total FSAT scores correlated slightly higher with SAT-Total than did the combined RAT and MAT score.

score and its corresponding FSAT score and (2) that the crosswalk and regression equation was stable. We tested the stability of the equations by randomly splitting the sample in half according to month of birth (students born on odd-numbered months in one group, even-numbered months in the other group), and repeated the calibrating process separately on the two halves. Results were very similar to those obtained for the full sample. Visual inspection of the degree of linear relationship, combined with this stability check, lead us to conclude that all three links (i.e., RAT to SAT-V, MAT to SAT-M, and FSAT-Total to SAT-Total) clearly passed both checks (see the appendix). Thus, we have a high degree of confidence in the accuracy of the links for the limited purpose of conducting the analyses described below.

MEAN SAT SCORES AT CUNY

Our analyses used SAT scores on the recently "re-centered" scale. This scale has a national mean of 500 on each test (1,000 on total score). Table 3.3 shows the estimated mean SAT-V, SAT-M, and SAT-Total scores for all entering CUNY freshmen in 1997 by which degree they were seeking. One benchmark for interpreting SAT scores is the National Collegiate Athletic association's eligibility requirements for athletic scholarships; namely, a student must have an SAT-Total score of at least 820 (and HSGPA of at least 2.5 in 13 core academic subjects).

Another benchmark is SAT scores at other colleges. Given CUNY's relatively modest admissions standards, it is not surprising that its SAT scores are fairly low compared with most other colleges in New York and nationally. For example, we identified four New York col-

Table 3.3

Estimated Mean SAT Scores of 1997 Freshmen

	Bachelor	Associate
Test	Degree	Degree
Verbal	447	402
Math	469	402
Total	916	799

leges from the annual *USNews* college rankings that were in the same tier (Northern Universities, Tier 2) as Brooklyn, Baruch, and Hunter. The SAT score ranges corresponding to 25th and 75th percentiles for these four colleges (College of New Rochelle, Iona College, SUNY Plattsburgh, and SUNY Oswego) were 890–1050, 910–1100, 960–1140, and 980–1180, respectively. In comparison, the 25th and 75th percentile points for CUNY's bachelor's students were 795 and 1040.

The mean total SAT scores of the June 1997 graduates who went to CUNY that fall were 817 for the 4,173 associate students and 910 for the 4,386 bachelor students. The corresponding means for other associate and bachelor students in this class were 796 and 926. These data indicate that the SAT scores of the 8,559 June 1997 graduates from New York City public schools who went to CUNY that fall were fairly comparable to the SAT scores of the other CUNY freshmen in this class.

Table 3.4 shows the mean SAT and FSAT scores at each college. Some schools (such as John Jay) are listed twice because they have large numbers of both bachelor and associate degree seeking–students. Within a degree, schools are listed in descending order of their SAT-Total scores. This sequence is almost identical to the order of their mean total FSAT scores, Probably because of the reliability problems discussed above, the mean RAT and MAT scores tracked SAT scores across schools much better than did mean WAT scores.

The mean total FSAT scores in Table 3.4 may not equal the sum of the mean RAT, MAT and WAT scores because these means are based on slightly different numbers of students (i.e., not all students have scores for all three tests). Missing data on one or more tests also affected the mean SAT-Total score, which was estimated (using their total FSAT score) for students who did not take the SATs. As a result, the mean SAT-Total score may not equal the sum of the means of the SAT-V and the SAT-M. In most cases, the difference is negligible. At Hostos, however, only 50 percent of the students took all three parts of the FSAT, and these students tended to have higher RAT and MAT scores than other Hostos students. The estimated mean SAT-Total score for Hostos is based on the subset of students with complete data and is therefore not representative of the entire freshman class.

Table 3.4

Mean SAT and FSAT Scores and Freshman GPA by Degree Sought and College for Students Entering in Fall 1997

Degree/College[a]	N	GPA	SAT Scores			FSAT Scores			
			Verbal	Math	Total	RAT	MAT	WAT	Total
Bachelor									
Baruch	1,082	2.33	464	501	968	33	32	7	72
Hunter	1,712	2.50	460	483	946	33	31	7	71
Queens	1,205	2.59	461	481	942	32	30	7	69
Staten Island	252	2.73	453	472	926	33	30	7	69
Brooklyn	1,368	2.30	449	479	924	31	29	7	67
City College	954	2.46	440	479	918	30	30	6	67
John Jay	904	2.31	438	426	864	31	26	7	63
York	464	2.35	410	441	847	28	27	6	61
Lehman	711	2.37	407	410	811	28	25	6	59
Associate									
Staten Island	1,440	2.22	438	422	859	31	24	7	61
Medgar Evers	527	2.11	415	403	810	28	22	6	56
Kingsborough	2,030	2.40	411	404	809	28	22	6	56
Queensborough	1,717	2.04	409	409	809	27	23	6	57
Manhattan	3,044	2.37	405	411	808	27	23	6	56
NYC Technical	2,170	2.13	400	408	800	27	23	6	56
John Jay	715	1.88	411	389	794	28	21	6	55
La Guardia	2,076	2.45	390	398	776	25	22	6	53
Hostos	671	2.44	328	340	747	20	16	6	50
Bronx	1,103	2.14	374	366	717	23	18	5	47

[a]Results are reported for each degree/college combination with over 50 students.

A more appropriate estimate of the mean SAT-Total score for Hostos is therefore the sum of its mean SAT-V and SAT-M scores (i.e., 668 rather than 747).

There are large differences in the general academic ability (as measured by SATs and FSATs) of the students attending different schools within the CUNY system. The top six colleges in Table 3.4 have much more able students (as measured by FSA and SAT-Total scores) than do the next three schools. For example, there is a very large (54-point) difference in mean SAT-Total scores between City College (the sixth school on the list) and John Jay (the seventh school). Similarly, Bronx, Hostos, and La Guardia had much lower mean SAT-Total scores than did other colleges, including other community colleges. Moreover, Staten Island's mean SAT score was substantially higher than the mean at the other community colleges granting associate degrees.

The large differences in mean student ability among schools (as measured by FSATs and SATs) do not correspond to differences in their grading standards. To illustrate, Table 3.4 shows that the mean GPA at Baruch, the school with the most academically able students, was lower than the mean GPA at six of the other senior colleges. It also was lower than the mean GPA at Hostos and at some of the other community colleges. These differences raise serious concerns about transferring grades and credits across CUNY's colleges.

RELATIONSHIP BETWEEN STUDENT DEMOGRAPHICS AND SAT SCORES

Figure 3.1 shows how SAT-Total scores of students seeking a bachelor's degree are related to their racial/ethnic group and primary language (English speakers versus English-language learners). Figure 3.2 shows the corresponding data for students seeking an associate degree. In both figures, each horizontal bar represents the middle 50 percent of the distribution of scores for a group. The left-hand side of each bar shows the 25th percentile within that group, the vertical line in the middle of the bar shows the 50th-percentile point, and the right-hand side of the bar shows the 75th-percentile point. For example, the bottom bar in Figure 3.1 shows that roughly the middle 50 percent of the black bachelor degree English-language learners had an SAT-Total score between 740 and 950. The median (50th-percentile point) in this group was just below 850. Figure 3.1 also shows that the middle 50 percent of the Asian bachelor degree English speakers had SAT scores between 900 and 1,140. The mean SAT score among all those who take the SAT nationally (i.e., among students who are aspiring to go to college) is about 1,000. The mean among all bachelor's students at CUNY was 916 (which is far below the national average).

Figures 3.1 and 3.2 show that within a racial/ethnic group, English speakers generally had much higher scores than English learners (as per the definitions of these groups used earlier in this report). When English fluency is held constant, Asian and white students generally

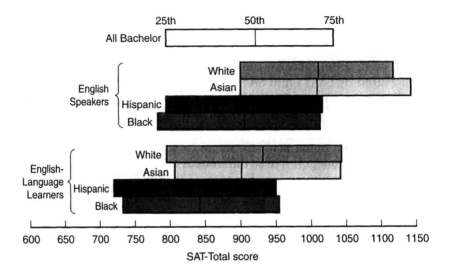

Figure 3.1—Interquartile Range by Racial/Ethnic Group for Bachelor Degree Students

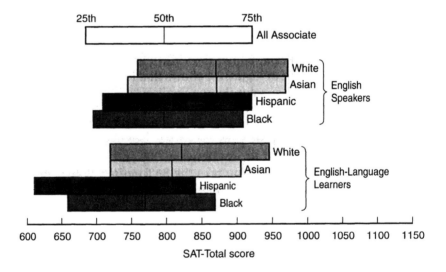

Figure 3.2—Interquartile Range by Racial/Ethnic Group for Associate Degree Students

had higher SAT-Total scores than their classmates (the bachelor and associate degree students in the "other" category had SAT score distributions that were comparable to the entire populations of bachelor and associate students, respectively; see the top bar in each figure). In fact, white and Asian English-language learners generally had scores that were as high or higher than those of Hispanics and blacks who were English speakers.

A comparison of Figures 3.1 and 3.2 shows that bachelor students tended to earn substantially higher SAT scores than associate students. For example, the 25th percentile among all bachelor students corresponded to an SAT score of 795, which is exactly equal to the median (50th percentile) score for associate students. Moreover, the median score for bachelor students (920) corresponded to the 75th percentile for associate students.

The differences in the distributions of SAT scores between certain racial/ethnic groups are comparable in size to the differences between bachelor's and associate students. For example, Figure 3.1 shows that among English speakers, about 75 percent of the white and Asian bachelor students had higher SAT scores than half of the black and Hispanic bachelor students. As discussed earlier in this report, this disparity is not due to the tests being biased against blacks or Hispanics.

POLICY IMPLICATIONS OF DIFFERENCES AMONG GROUPS

Figure 3.1 shows that if CUNY raised its admission standards for bachelor degree students at some or all of its senior colleges, then the percentages of black and Hispanic students who would reach these standards would most likely be lower than the percentages of Asian and white students who would meet them. Thus, at least in the short term, the data suggest that raising standards would result in the most selective schools having disproportionately fewer black and Hispanic students than Asian and white students. This situation could, of course, be mitigated if CUNY adopted an affirmative action policy that involved imposing substantially higher standards for whites and Asians than it employed for blacks and Hispanics. We do not discuss in this report the public policy and political consequences of using different admission standards for different groups to ensure racial balance in access to CUNY colleges.

It is difficult to predict the long-term consequences of higher admission standards on racial disparities. For example, higher standards could lead to improved academic preparation of black and Hispanic students (i.e., before they come to CUNY), which in turn could raise their college graduation rates. Thus, higher standards could lead to raising the net number of blacks and Hispanics who graduate from CUNY. Shifting the policy focus from access to college to graduation rates could therefore lead to different decisions regarding the appropriateness of imposing higher admission standards on all students.

Finally, there appears to be no other factor (besides racial/ethnic group) that can be inserted into the admissions process that will lead to racial/ethnic balance. For example, the admissions office at UCLA found that including a student's socioeconomic status in the admissions process will not come close to restoring the racial/ethnic balance that was achieved by the affirmative action policies that were in place prior to the implementation of Prop. 209, the proposition that eliminated racial/ethnic group from the admissions process (Doby, W., Vice Chancellor, personal communication). To achieve such balance, at least in the short run, the admissions process will either have to consider the student's racial/ethnic group or substantially lower admissions standards. There is no way around this. In addition, policymakers will have to develop guidelines for defining what constitutes "balance." For example, must a racial/ethnic group's share of the student body at a college equal its share among all high school graduates in New York City, among all CUNY students, etc.? If so, then this would essentially raise admission standards for whites and Asians, but not for blacks and Hispanics.

Chapter Four

ANALYSIS OF HIGH SCHOOL DATA

Although there are over a million school children in New York City's public schools, only about 30,000 graduate from high school each spring. About 8,600 of these students (29 percent) went to CUNY and of this group (96 percent) took at least one Regents English or mathematics exam. The 18,551 non–CUNY-bound June 1997 high school graduates who also took at least one Regents exam had a moderately (and statistically significant) higher mean score on these exams than did those who went to CUNY. The difference was about one quarter of a standard deviation unit on each test. The gender and racial/ethnic composition of the CUNY-bound students was very similar to the composition of the non–CUNY-bound students. Taken together, these data suggest that the more able college-bound high school graduates from New York City's public schools were somewhat more likely to go someplace other than CUNY, but the difference was not dramatic.

Within CUNY itself, the students in the cohort of 8,559 Spring 1997 high school graduates were much more likely to seek a bachelor's degree than were the 15,870 Fall 1997 CUNY freshmen who were not recent New York City public high school graduates. The percentages in these two groups were 51 percent and 21 percent, respectively. However, within a degree track, the Spring 1997 and non–Spring 1997 graduates had very similar test scores and demographic characteristics. For example, among those seeking a bachelor's degree, their respective mean RAT scores were 31.1 and 31.4; their mean SAT-M scores were 466 and 472; and their corresponding percentages of English speakers were 48 percent and 52 percent. This similarity suggests that once degree type is controlled for, the relationship of CUNY GPAs to high school grades and test scores in the cohort of Spring 1997 high school graduates is likely to be similar to the relationship between these variables in the population of all entering CUNY students (but this should be checked by further research because results could be influenced by factors that we were not able to control).

We used the cohort of 8,559 June 1997 New York public high school graduates who went to CUNY that fall to examine how first-year grades at CUNY were related to high school grades and to the scores on the English and mathematics portion of the New York State Regents exams (hereafter referred to as "Regents"). This was done by constructing 12 regression equations for bachelor degree students and another 12 for associate degree students.

All 12 equations contained the same set of background and demographic characteristics; namely, racial/ethnic group, language (English-language learner versus English speaker), and college. The latter variable was included to help compensate for differences in grading standards across schools within CUNY. The 12 models differed with respect to whether they included one or more of the following variables: SATs (SAT-V and SAT-M), FSATs (RAT, MAT, and WAT), high school grade point average (HSGPA), and score on the Regents English and math exams.

Table 4.1 shows the squared multiple correlation (R-square) for each model for each group (comparisons can be made between these data and those in Tables 2.4 and 2.5 by squaring the correlation coefficients in those tables). The R-square value is an index of the extent to which differences in first-year grades among students can be explained by differences in their background characteristics and test scores (i.e., by the variables in the model). Specifically, an R-square value indicates the proportion of the variance in the students' grades that can be accounted for by the variance in these students' predictor scores.

In general, the R-square for predicting freshman grades from high school grades and admissions test scores is in the .10–.15 range (prior to any adjustment for restriction in range). Values over .20 are definitely above average. Table 4.1 shows that combining Regents scores and/or HSGPAs with a student's FSAT or SAT scores yields a more accurate prediction of a student's likelihood of success at CUNY than does using any of these measures by themselves. In fact, the highest R-squares are obtained by combining HSGPA with two of the three sets of test scores. However, as we saw in Tables 2.4 and 2.5, the predictor variables are much more accurate in estimating first-year grades for bachelor degree students than they are for predicting the grades of associate degree students.

Table 4.1

R-Squares of Various Models in Predicting Freshman GPAs

Model Number	Variables in the Model	Bachelor ($N = 4,429$)	Associate ($N = 4,069$)
1	Covariates (school, language, and race)	.06	.06
2	Covariates + Regents	.14	.11
3	Covariates + HSGPA	.17	.07
4	Covariates + HSGPA + Regents	.20	.11
5	Covariates + SATs	.10	.07
6	Covariates + SATs + Regents	.14	.11
7	Covariates + SATs + HSGPA	.20	.08
8	Covariates + SATs + HSGPA + Regents	.21	.11
9	Covariates + FSATs	.12	.08
10	Covariates + FSATs + Regents	.15	.11
11	Covariates + FSATs + HSGPA	.21	.08
12	Covariates + FSATs + HSGPA + Regents	.22	.11

Chapter Five

ADDITIONAL RESEARCH ACTIVITIES

This chapter first notes some of our concerns with CUNY's database. We then discuss several research studies that would provide useful information if CUNY retains its current testing program or launches a new one.

IMPROVE DATA QUALITY

While conducting the analyses for Chapters Two and Three of this report, we encountered some questionable data. For example, key demographic information was missing for a large percentage of students, and several students had more than 35 credits in their freshman year (and one had 46 credits even though it is highly unlikely that a student took a dozen or more courses over two semesters).

In addition, our discussions with CUNY staff indicated that in the fall of 1997, two WAT forms were used (forms 33 and 34). However, the computer file for the freshmen entering in 1997 had codes for over 50 different forms! The number of students answering forms 33 and 34 were 7,422 and 5,320, respectively, out of 23,300 takers (1,129 students did not have a WAT score). These data suggest that only slightly more than 50 percent of the students took one of the two forms that were presumably administered to everyone. We do not know whether these results stem from clerical/keystroking errors or problems with the documentation for the electronic files we received, or whether they signal more significant and pervasive problems. Whatever the reason, it is evident that CUNY needs to improve the quality of its student information system.

ANALYZE HIGH SCHOOL DATA

The combination of SAT or FSAT scores with high school grades or Regents scores provides a more accurate prediction of a student's college grades than do any of these variables by themselves. In addition, measurement specialists generally recommend using more than one test score to make important decisions about individual students. In light of such considerations, we suggest that CUNY determine whether using high school data (including scores on statewide tests) would improve the assessment of a student's readiness for college-level work at CUNY. We began to explore this matter in Chapter Four of this report, but a more thorough analysis is required, particularly since we were only able to look at about one-third of the CUNY freshmen.

DOCUMENT BASIS FOR PASS/FAIL STANDARDS

As noted in Chapter Two of this report, there does not appear to be any documented empirical or theoretical basis for the passing scores CUNY selected for the RAT, MAT, and WAT. In addition, these tests have very different passing rates. Consequently, if these tests are to be retained, we strongly recommend that research be conducted to determine what the passing score on each test should be.

ASSESS THE CONSISTENCY OF CUNY'S GRADING STANDARDS

The relatively low correlations of both SAT and FSAT scores with CUNY GPAs of associate degree students may stem at least in part from problems with the grading system; i.e., the outcome variable may not be very reliable. If so, it could depress the correlation of CUNY GPAs with other measures. A study of the reliability of grades at CUNY could therefore isolate the source(s) of the low correlations between GPAs and test scores.

In addition, the data in Table 3.4 suggested that there were large differences in grading standards across CUNY's colleges (e.g., the schools with the most academically able students—as measured by FSAT and SAT scores—did not have the highest average GPAs). Research on CUNY's grading policies and practices would help to identify the sources of these inconsistencies and provide insights into how they could be eliminated so as to increase the fairness of the grades and facilitate their transfer across schools.

A more in-depth analysis also could examine the degree to which grading standards at CUNY are comparable to those at other colleges. This type of research might involve administering a common set of test questions as part of final course exams to students from different schools within and outside of CUNY, giving standardized high school advanced placement tests to CUNY students at the end of comparable first-year courses, and similar strategies.

EVALUATE THE EFFECTIVENESS OF DIFFERENT REMEDIAL PROGRAMS

Almost every freshman associate degree student and two out of three entering bachelor degree students receive remedial instruction at CUNY. Some of the remedial programs are no doubt more cost-effective than others, as indicated by the amount of time and other resources they require to help students reach the level of verbal and mathematical proficiency CUNY students need to do college work. Thus, it would be useful to determine which programs or program types are most effective for which types of students. This research should include some non-FSAT measures of student proficiency because many of the remedial courses now use the FSATs as part of their instructional program.

DEVELOP VALID AND APPROPRIATE SYSTEMWIDE MEASURES OF STUDENT ABILITIES

All CUNY graduates should master certain basic reading, math, and writing skills. That is why CUNY instituted the FSATs, and according to its own standards on these tests, a very large percentage of its incoming students require remedial instruction. However, CUNY has no systematic way of assessing whether the remedial instruction that was given to these students was effective; i.e., whether its graduates actually possess the requisite skills.

CUNY's proposed "60th credit" (single-question essay) exam will not assess mastery of the relevant basic abilities because it does not assess math or science skills. It also suffers from the same score reliability problems as the WAT. Hence, we suggest that CUNY consider developing or adopting a valid system of secure tests for assessing whether its students have acquired the basic skills that are commensurate with a bachelor and associate degree. We also suggest that CUNY begin formally monitoring and reporting upon the success of its graduates on relevant licensing and certification tests, such as for teachers and accountants, as one factor in assessing the quality of its instructional programs in these areas.

EXAMINE THE "VALUE ADDED" OF A CUNY DEGREE

The "value added" of an institution of higher learning is measured by the degree to which its students are eventually substantially better off (in terms of income, job and life satisfaction, etc.) than are similarly situated individuals who did not go to CUNY. For example, does going to CUNY lead to securing a better job, becoming more productive, etc.? CUNY could answer these and related questions by conducting a longitudinal study of a stratified random sample of the students who enrolled in a given year (e.g., Fall 1992) to find out what they are doing now, their thoughts about the quality of the education they received, and similar matters.

Chapter Six

POLICY OPTIONS AND RECOMMENDATIONS

CUNY must decide whether to maintain its generally modest admissions standards. If it retains these standards, then it will have to do two things: (1) provide effective remedial instruction to large numbers of students at both the senior and community colleges and (2) have a defensible method for determining which students receive that instruction.

Another strategy would be to raise admission standards at some or all of the other senior colleges and channel those students requiring remedial instruction to the community colleges and/or other public or private programs. The rationale for this strategy is that it would more efficiently serve the needs of students who need remedial assistance as well as raise academic standards. This will also increase the prestige of the CUNY system and thereby potentially attract more able students to its colleges. If this approach is adopted, then CUNY will need a valid and appropriate set of criteria for setting cut scores and determining which students should go to which schools.

The results presented in this report indicate that in deciding between these and other options, CUNY will need to keep in mind several factors, including the following:

It may not be appropriate for CUNY to continue to use the FSATs to make high-stakes decisions, such as whether a student is required to take a remedial course or can be admitted to a particular college. The major reasons for this concern are (1) the security of the RAT and MAT has been breached and (2) the score reliability of the WAT is far below what is appropriate for making important decisions about individual students. It is just not adequate for the task it is being asked to perform, especially since it is the major determinant of whether a student is required to take a remedial course.

Although writing skills are certainly important to measure, the WAT cannot be trusted to provide an accurate index of those skills. In addition, scoring costs alone on this test are about $200,000 per year. Hence, if CUNY continues its FSAT program, then it should (1) base the WAT score on several essay questions per student and/or (2) combine the WAT and RAT scores into a composite "total language arts" score. In addition, CUNY should go through a formal standard-setting process and analysis to determine the appropriate passing ("cut") score on each component test in the FSAT program.

If CUNY decides to impose stricter admission standards for bachelor students at some of its senior colleges, then, at least in the short term, white and Asian students will have a much higher likelihood of being admitted than will students from most other racial or ethnic groups. These differences stem from black and Hispanic students tending to have lower (and sometimes substantially lower) admissions credentials than their classmates (see Figures 3.1 and 3.2). These disparities are not due to problems in the tests. Specifically, our analyses found that the differences in average test scores between groups did not stem from gross differences in English fluency rates between groups or from the tests being biased against black or Hispanic students. In fact, we found that the tests actually favored these students in the sense that their actual GPAs at CUNY were statistically significantly lower than what would be predicted on the basis of their FSAT or SAT scores, while the reverse was true for Asian and white students.

Finally, Chapter Five of this report listed several areas in which CUNY might conduct additional research. These areas include conducting further investigations of the utility of using high school grades in making selection and placement decisions, assessing the reliability and appropriateness of CUNY's grading and curriculum standards, evaluating the effectiveness of various remedial programs for different types of students, instituting a quality control check on basic skills, and examining the "value added" of a CUNY degree.

STATISTICAL DATA

Table A.1

Results of RAT Reliability Analysis

Cronbach coefficient alpha for raw variables	0.889312
Cronbach coefficient alpha for standardized variables	0.891348

Deleted Variable	Raw Variables		Standardized Variables	
	Correlation with Total	Alpha	Correlation with Total	Alpha
Item 01	0.450136	0.885866	0.453901	0.887947
Item 02	0.330599	0.887827	0.338122	0.889613
Item 03	0.322419	0.887743	0.327721	0.889761
Item 04	0.488465	0.885422	0.493883	0.887367
Item 05	0.401629	0.886691	0.406865	0.888626
Item 06	0.383578	0.886827	0.383626	0.888961
Item 07	0.437624	0.886077	0.443585	0.888096
Item 08	0.384987	0.886914	0.390559	0.888861
Item 09	0.259312	0.888746	0.259190	0.890737
Item 10	0.391690	0.886832	0.396778	0.888771
Item 11	0.314483	0.887856	0.317349	0.889910
Item 12	0.384706	0.886832	0.387304	0.888908
Item 13	0.302946	0.887934	0.307172	0.890055
Item 14	0.397982	0.886604	0.399352	0.888734
Item 15	0.361581	0.887201	0.359543	0.889306
Item 16	0.306394	0.888071	0.303542	0.890106
Item 17	0.348162	0.887371	0.347825	0.889474
Item 18	0.151740	0.890449	0.150164	0.892274
Item 19	0.299077	0.888155	0.294670	0.890233
Item 20	0.197278	0.889366	0.193508	0.891665
Item 21	0.479729	0.885386	0.483231	0.887522
Item 22	0.327247	0.887731	0.329356	0.889738

Table A.1 (continued)

Deleted Variable	Raw Variables		Standardized Variables	
	Correlation with Total	Alpha	Correlation with Total	Alpha
Item 23	0.477501	0.885504	0.481734	0.887544
Item 24	0.373307	0.887003	0.377173	0.889053
Item 25	0.312349	0.887973	0.310439	0.890008
Item 26	0.330806	0.887644	0.334679	0.889662
Item 27	0.404070	0.886622	0.408807	0.888598
Item 28	0.421097	0.886618	0.426745	0.888340
Item 29	0.539278	0.884497	0.541899	0.886667
Item 30	0.356283	0.887239	0.359808	0.889302
Item 31	0.320769	0.887858	0.317870	0.889902
Item 32	0.394750	0.886655	0.389253	0.888880
Item 33	0.421566	0.886215	0.416735	0.888484
Item 34	0.286281	0.888426	0.283855	0.890387
Item 35	0.485592	0.885327	0.485980	0.887482
Item 36	0.421284	0.886220	0.416976	0.888481
Item 37	0.419806	0.886260	0.418705	0.888456
Item 38	0.472804	0.885531	0.472755	0.887674
Item 39	0.452649	0.885721	0.449718	0.888008
Item 40	0.286339	0.888408	0.284085	0.890383
Item 41	0.503616	0.884857	0.499181	0.887290
Item 42	0.509447	0.884958	0.507955	0.887162
Item 43	0.257573	0.888831	0.252443	0.890832
Item 44	0.261633	0.888614	0.256485	0.890775
Item 45	0.225542	0.889200	0.220645	0.891282

Table A.2

Results of MAT Reliability Analysis

Cronbach coefficient alpha for raw variables   0.894655
Cronbach coefficient alpha for standardized variables   0.892351

Deleted Variable	Raw Variables		Standardized Variables	
	Correlation with Total	Alpha	Correlation with Total	Alpha
Item 01	0.235997	0.894527	0.238097	0.892253
Item 02	0.063013	0.895595	0.065885	0.894863
Item 03	0.340882	0.893050	0.344046	0.890621
Item 04	0.515323	0.890316	0.512129	0.887993
Item 05	0.372716	0.892608	0.377389	0.890104
Item 06	0.382619	0.892475	0.382947	0.890017
Item 07	0.251150	0.894625	0.255339	0.891989
Item 08	0.472990	0.890994	0.468169	0.888685
Item 09	0.559159	0.889778	0.558557	0.887258
Item 10	0.422850	0.891812	0.423526	0.889384
Item 11	0.376689	0.892554	0.372757	0.890176
Item 12	0.290049	0.893792	0.292050	0.891424
Item 13	0.278043	0.893873	0.284294	0.891544
Item 14	0.330802	0.893145	0.334827	0.890764
Item 15	0.362045	0.892743	0.362092	0.890341
Item 16	0.284403	0.893770	0.289325	0.891466
Item 17	0.370357	0.892680	0.369517	0.890226
Item 18	0.193780	0.894535	0.199142	0.892848
Item 19	0.511086	0.890346	0.506553	0.888081
Item 20	0.347050	0.892947	0.353859	0.890469
Item 21	0.565286	0.889549	0.562226	0.887199
Item 22	0.447553	0.891436	0.447608	0.889007
Item 23	0.548854	0.889933	0.547609	0.887431
Item 24	0.401064	0.892172	0.401374	0.889730
Item 25	0.547737	0.889891	0.544802	0.887476
Item 26	0.464176	0.891163	0.462266	0.888778
Item 27	0.427623	0.891734	0.425148	0.889359
Item 28	0.569727	0.889554	0.565205	0.887152
Item 29	0.283716	0.894072	0.281212	0.891591
Item 30	0.468588	0.891056	0.462243	0.888778
Item 31	0.396411	0.892557	0.398836	0.889770
Item 32	0.516099	0.890288	0.511696	0.887999
Item 33	0.389378	0.892340	0.391722	0.889881
Item 34	0.427349	0.891739	0.422547	0.889400
Item 35	0.317813	0.893533	0.317226	0.891036
Item 36	0.437013	0.891579	0.432544	0.889243
Item 37	0.484328	0.890801	0.480621	0.888489
Item 38	0.437823	0.891565	0.432376	0.889246
Item 39	0.229594	0.894942	0.226459	0.892431
Item 40	0.362361	0.892796	0.357514	0.890412

Table A.3

Mean Freshman GPAs and Residual Scores by Racial/Ethnic Group and Degree for Four Models

Degree/ Ethnicity	N	Actual GPA	Mean Residual Score for			
			FSAT Model 1	FSAT Model 2	FSAT Model 3	FSAT Model 4
Bachelor						
White	1,940	2.61	.12**	.13**	.12**	.12**
Black	1,477	2.31	−.04*	−.03	−.04	−.02
Hispanic	1,834	2.23	−.16**	−.14**	−.15**	−.13**
Asian	1,232	2.53	.06*	.01	.05*	.00
Other	900	2.48	.04	.04	.04	.05
Associate						
White	2,206	2.43	.14**	.15**	.15**	.16**
Black	3,821	2.13	−.08**	−.07**	−.08**	−.08**
Hispanic	3,505	2.17	−.07**	−.06**	−.07**	−.05**
Asian	1,018	2.56	.22**	.13**	.22**	.14**
Other	1,835	2.28	.00	.00	.00	.00

* = significant at .05; ** = significant at .001.

NOTES: Residual score = Actual GPA −·Predicted GPA. The R-Squares for models 1–4 were .07, .08, .07, and .08, respectively. The dependent variable for all four models was the students' freshman GPA. In addition to degree, all four models also included dummy variables for primary language (English speaker versus English-language learner), and college. The models differed in terms of their other predictor variables as follows: Model 1 used FSAT total score (i.e., RAT + MAT + WAT); model 2 used each of these three tests as separate variables; model 3 used SAT-Total score; and model 4 used SAT-V and SAT-M scores as separate variables. Where necessary, SAT scores were imputed from FSAT scores using the procedures described in Chapter Three of this report. The tabled N's are for the FSAT models (and they are about 99 percent of the N's in the SAT models).

Table A.4

FSAT-SAT Crosswalk

Percentile	FSATs	SAT-Total	RAT	SAT-V	MAT	SAT-M
5	35	590	14	260	11	280
10	41	640	17	310	14	320
15	44	680	19	330	15	340
20	47	720	21	350	17	350
25	50	740	23	360	18	370
30	52	770	24	380	20	380
35	54	790	25	390	21	400
40	56	810	27	400	22	410
45	58	830	28	410	24	420
50	60	860	29	430	25	430
55	62	880	30	440	26	450
60	64	910	31	450	27	460
65	66	930	32	460	29	470
70	68	960	34	480	30	490
75	70	980	35	490	31	500
80	73	1020	36	510	33	520
85	75	1050	37	530	34	550
90	78	1100	39	560	35	580
95	82	1190	40	600	37	620

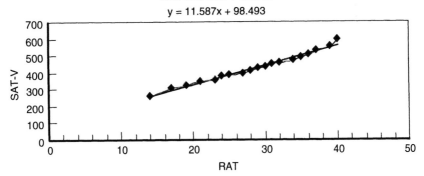

**Equi-percentile equating of
RAT and SAT-V scores**

$y = 11.587x + 98.493$

Figure A.1—Relationship Between RAT Total Score and SAT-V

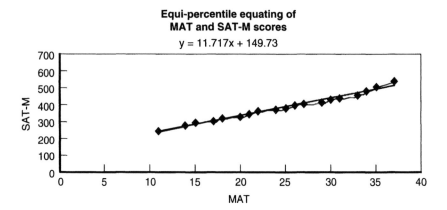

Figure A.2—Relationship Between MAT Total Score and SAT-M

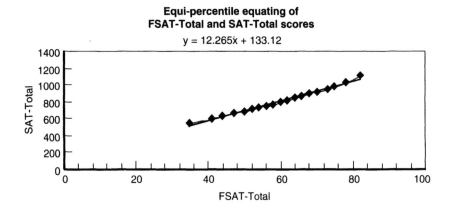

Figure A.3—Relationship Between FSAT Total Score and SAT Total Score

Table A.5

Crosswalk Equations for Full Sample and Random Halves

	Verbal	Math	Total
		Crosswalk Relationship	
Full sample	y = 11.6x + 98	y = 11.7x + 149	y = 12.3x + 133
Half 1	y = 11.6x + 98	y = 11.6x + 150	y = 12.0x + 145
Half 2	y = 11.8x + 94	y = 11.9x + 142	y = 12.2x + 137

BIBLIOGRAPHY

American Educational Research Association, American Psychological Association, and National Council on Measurement in Education. *Standards for Educational and Psychological Testing*, Washington, D.C.: American Psychological Association, 1985.

College Board, *Counselors Handbook for the SAT Program 1998–1999*. New York, 1999.

Crocker, L. M., and J. Algina, *Introduction to Classical and Modern Test Theory*, New York: Holt, Rinehart and Winston, 1986, pp. 226–227.

Dunbar, S., D. Koretz, and H. D. Hoover, "Quality Control in the Development and Use of Performance Assessment," *Applied Measurement in Education*, Vol. 4, No. 4, 1991, pp. 289–303.

Gill, Brian P., *The Governance of the City University of New York*, Santa Monica, Calif.: RAND, MR-1141-EDU, 2000.

Office of Academic Affairs, CUNY, "The CUNY Writing Assessment Test: Audit Results 1988–97," 1998.

Otheguy, R., "The Condition of Latinos in the City University of New York." A report to the Vice Chancellor for Academic Affairs and to the Puerto Rican Council on Higher Education. Unpublished report, 1990.

The Mayor's Advisory Task Force on the City University of New York, *CUNY A System Adrift*. Office of the Mayor, 1999.